PAPER IT

Dek Messecar
Series Consultant Editor: Bob Tattersall

CONTENTS

COLLINS

Introduction

Wallpaper was invented as a cheap way of applying designs to walls. Since then, there has been produced a huge variety of other materials (such as fabric, metal foil, cork, wood, yarn, plastics, grasses, felt, glass fibre, etc.) whose purposes range from mere decoration to insulation, sound deadening, fire retarding, light control and improving a surface before decorating.

This book will help you find your way through the maze of products that have become known as wall coverings. There are colour illustrations to give you ideas about how they can be used, and straightforward instructions to show you how to hang them yourself.

Right *The striking design of this wallpaper is repeated in the fabric which has been draped over the table for an attractive, coordinated effect. The colours chosen echo those in the painting.*

Above *Lightweight wallpaper lends a delicate atmosphere to bedrooms. This traditional pattern creates an authentic setting for the old furniture and picture frames.*

Left *These walls and ceiling have been covered with striped fabric on a paper backing. To disguise the joins between ceiling and wall, a wood cornice has been put up after the wall covering.*

3

TOOLS AND MATERIALS

Here is a checklist of the tools and materials you will find mentioned later in this section. Each item is followed by a brief description or explanation of its purpose. How many tools you will need depends on the type of wall covering you choose and also on how large a job you're going to tackle. For a small papering job, the minimum would be wallpapering scissors, plumb line, hanging brush, pasting brush, metal straight edge, and trimming knife. You will also need a supply of sponges, cloths, newspapers and a few plastic buckets.

Don't skimp on materials such as adhesives, sizes and fillers. Always use the type recommended by the wall covering manufacturer and follow the specific instructions about drying times.

Pasting table: Any table with a wipe clean surface will do, but a folding, purpose-made pasting table is easier to move around and keep near the work. It should be at least 2 metres long and longer if possible.

Pasting brushes and rollers: A proprietary pasting brush is better than a paint brush as the bristles are coarser and stiffer. It is important to spread adhesives as evenly as possible as any lumps or ridges may show in the surface of the wall covering.

An ordinary short pile roller may be used when the job calls for pasting the wall rather than the wall covering. A normal paint tray is best for loading the roller.

Hanging brush: These, also, are made for the purpose and it is best not to use a substitute.

Use the brush for smoothing down paper and vinyl coverings and also for pushing folds into corners. Choose the largest brush that you can comfortably handle.

Felt and rubber rollers: Soft rollers are needed for smoothing fabrics, metal foil, and veneer coverings.

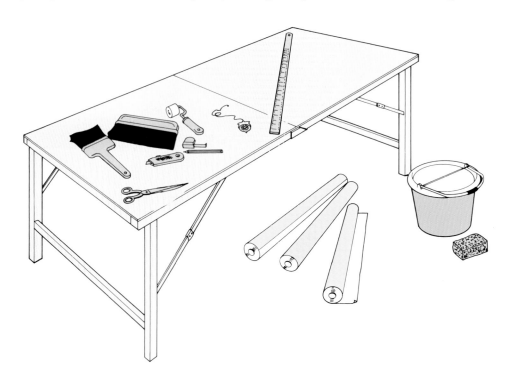

Seam rollers: These are hard plastic wheels approximately 25mm wide that are used to flatten joins between lengths of paper or vinyl. This is done when the adhesive is set but not yet hard. They should not be used on embossed papers, foils or fabrics.

Trimming knife: Choose a knife with replaceable blades, as a sharp edge is essential. Curved blades are best for wall covering materials.

Straight edge: A metal straight edge, such as a steel rule, is necessary for cutting straight lines, usually through two overlapping layers of material, to produce a butt join.

Shears: Don't be tempted to use household scissors. Paperhanging shears are shaped to crease paper into corners for marking and have edges designed for cutting wall covering materials.

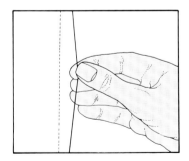

Chalk line: A reel of non stretch string that is used for marking straight lines. It is held taut against marks on the wall or ceiling, pulled away from the surface near the centre, and allowed to snap back, leaving a straight line of chalk.

Plumb line: This is a string with a weight on the end, used to mark vertical lines on walls. Any small object (such as a nut or washer) may be used as a plumb bob. The best bobs are flat so they can hang near the wall without touching, making accurate positioning easier. The line can be rubbed with chalk and used as described above.

Scrapers: Stiff, wide metal blades with handles, used to strip old wallpaper and loose paint during preparation. There are also modern scrapers of various shapes for different purposes.

Filling knives: These look like scrapers, but the blades are

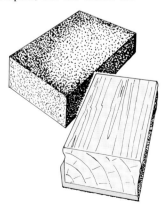

flexible. They are used to apply filler to holes, dents and cracks in walls and ceilings.

Sanding block and abrasives: The only sanding down that you will have to do before hanging wall coverings is when you fill cracks and holes or when papering over gloss paint. On flat areas, always wrap the abrasive paper around a wood, cork or rubber sanding block.

There is a wide range of modern sanding blocks available that help getting into awkward corners and edges and also abrasive-coated sponge blocks that can be rinsed in water during use to prevent clogging. Glasspaper or aluminium oxide coated paper is sufficient for preparing surfaces for most wall coverings.

Metal foil wall coverings need a very smooth surface as they show every flaw in the surface beneath. Fill any cracks carefully and rub down well with fine grade 'wet and dry' abrasives. These are cloth (instead of paper) backed and are rinsed in water frequently during use to avoid clogging.

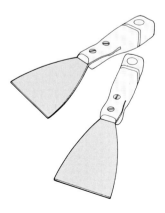

Fillers: If you have cracks and holes in the walls or ceiling, you will need to fill them. Even hairline cracks will show through the wall covering eventually. The best filling compounds are resin based rather than cellulose based. These are available ready to use or as a powder to be mixed with water and have the advantage of not shrinking as they harden. Instructions for using filler appear in the *Preparation* section of the book.

Pastes, adhesives and sizes: Different wall coverings need different adhesives. Lightweight papers use a cold water paste, but waterproof papers and vinyls need a paste that contains fungicide to prevent mould growth beneath the wall covering.

If you apply lining paper under a waterproof paper or vinyl wall covering, then the lining paper must also be hung with paste containing fungicide.

The rule to follow with adhesives is to choose the wall covering before the paste. The manufacturers' instructions will usually state which type of adhesive to use, and the instructions on the adhesive will specify the correct 'size'. .

Size is applied to surfaces during preparation to take up all excess absorbency. This prevents the adhesive soaking in and leaving 'dry spots' under the wall covering.

Chemical wallpaper strippers: When removing old wallpaper, these jellied water-based compounds cling better and dry more slowly than water. They are only necessary when the

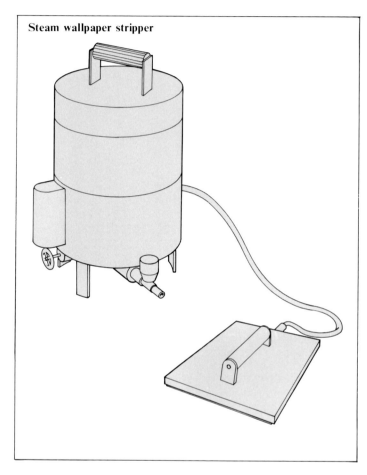

Steam wallpaper stripper

soak and scrape method (described in the *Preparation* section) is ineffective. However, they are less effective than steam wallpaper strippers. *Steam wallpaper strippers* are labour saving machines for removing wallpaper. They are inexpensive to hire and are widely available.

Primer/sealer: Primer may be necessary to prepare a newly plastered wall or ceiling that hasn't been decorated before, or

any areas of filler used to repair cracks and holes. You can use common oil-based primer, usually used to prepare wood or plaster for decorating, or water-based acrylic primers are available. These have the advantage of drying more quickly and not causing the smell common to oil paint.

Masonry sealer: Common primer for cement, concrete or brick that controls dust and neutralizes alkali that could effect wall covering adhesives.

Using Steps and Ladders Safely

Before tackling the job you have in mind, give some thought to the problem of reaching it. Take the time to make good arrangements to reach the work; it can mean the difference between a satisfying job and a frustrating (and dangerous) experience.

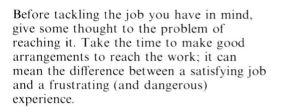

Low walls will require only a pair of steps, but papering a ceiling needs a platform running the full width of the room.

The most difficult area to work in is usually the stair well. It is possible to hire purpose built ladder systems for stairs, or you can use an arrangement of long ladder, step ladder and planks.

Planks that span a distance greater than 1.5 metres should have a second plank secured on top of them for safety.

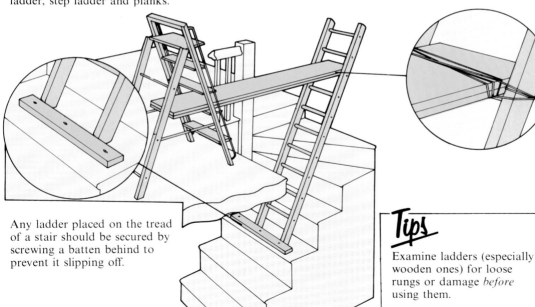

Any ladder placed on the tread of a stair should be secured by screwing a batten behind to prevent it slipping off.

Tips

Examine ladders (especially wooden ones) for loose rungs or damage *before* using them.

Don't stand too high on a ladder—keep your waist below the top rung.

WALL COVERINGS

When buying a wall covering, the first consideration (apart from price) is how much wear and tear the covering will be expected to take. This includes being rubbed by passing traffic in halls and stairs, and the cleaning required in different situations, such as kitchens and bathrooms.

Look around the walls for the places that get the most wear, and choose a wall covering that can take that kind of treatment without losing its looks.

You can use borders to break up walls and use different wall coverings above and below the border. For instance, a heavy washable or painted paper below the border will resist scuffing and dirt and the wall above the border (where wear is light) can be covered with a more fragile (or cheaper) covering.

Bear in mind that moist rooms (such as kitchens and bathrooms) must have a waterproof covering to resist condensation.

Types of wall coverings

Standard papers are the least expensive and one of the more fragile coverings. This is true both when hanging them and afterwards. They are not cleanable, but they can give a delicate atmosphere to bedrooms and spare rooms.

Heavy duty papers are made in several layers, sometimes embossed (textured), and are more durable.

Washables (often called 'vinyl-coated' wallpapers; not to be confused with paper-backed vinyls) are heavy duty papers that have been coated with a clear water-resistant surface that can be wiped (but not scrubbed) clean. This is also useful when hanging them, as paste can be easily removed from the surface without marking. Once hung, these papers are quite difficult to remove.

Very heavy papers are available either with wood chips for maximum disguise of surface faults or deeply embossed patterns that imitate tiles, rough plaster, pebbledash, etc. These papers are usually painted after hang-

ing and are very hard wearing. They are excellent for areas that may get damaged as they can be re-painted and even filled to look as good as new. A word of warning, however: once painted, they are very difficult to remove.

Other varieties of wallpaper include *ready-pasted papers* (adhesive applied during manufacture) that only require dipping in water before hanging, *dry-strip papers* that can be removed by pulling them off without soaking and scraping, and *flocked papers* that have patterns of raised velvet-like pile, usually in

Left *A tiny attic room is given style by an all-over treatment of standard wallpaper. Painting the beams instead of papering them helps to set off the pattern.*

Left *Here is the effect of using a painted heavy paper below to take the hard wear and standard wallpaper above, separated by a wood moulding.*

Right *Suede is a luxury wall covering that needs very careful hanging and should only be used where there will be little chance of it being touched.*

traditional designs. Flocks are difficult to hang because the pile is easily marked by adhesive or pressure.

Vinyl wall coverings are medium to heavy weight and consist of a layer of vinyl (on which the pattern is printed) over a paper backing. Vinyls are hard wearing and can be scrubbed, so they are perfect for kitchens, bathrooms, hallways, childrens' rooms, etc. Their patterns and colours are similar to wallpapers, though they are also available in plain colours with textured surfaces to sim-

ulate fabrics, cork or even tiles. There are flock vinyls and also metallic finish vinyls, and many are ready-pasted.

Although they are usually more expensive than paper, vinyls are probably the most practical (and easiest to hang) wall coverings as they don't tear easily and may be washed clean. However, the fact that they are water-proof means you have to use an adhesive containing a fungicide to prevent mould growth underneath them. Also, any overlapping of vinyl over vinyl requires a special glue.

Painting heavyweight paper (here, below the dado rail) with oil-based paint makes it highly durable.

Reflective finishes like this metal foil wall covering help to create a feeling of space.

The instructions on the rolls will usually specify what type to use.

Fabrics have long been used, but pasting them to walls is a difficult task and the results can be disappointing. However, most fabrics are available trimmed and mounted on paper backing, and may be hung as wallpaper, though some require special adhesives and techniques do vary. Hessian, silk, linen, woven grasses, felt, wool yarns and real cork fall into this category. Bear in mind that natural materials are affected by sunlight and colours can fade unevenly. Also, these materials are much more expensive than paper or plastics, and more easily spoiled during hanging, so gain experience with other types before attempting them.

Glass fibre in random weave is a very strong covering that can be used to hide and reinforce cracked walls.

Wood veneer on a heavy canvas backing can be used to achieve a panelled room effect.

Deep relief panels of a putty-like compound on a very heavy paper backing are made to simulate fabric, stone, brick, tiles and fielded wood panelling.

Metal foils are available in a variety of striking designs and colours. Unlike the vinyl metallics, however, they need careful handling, damage easily, are not washable, and show every slight defect in the surface beneath.

Borders are decorative strips that may be used to separate different wall coverings or finish edges in partially papered rooms i.e. to create the effect of a picture rail, frieze, cornice or dado.

Estimating for Wall Coverings

Before shopping for wall coverings, estimate how much you will need. It is important to buy enough, as most coverings are made in batches and colour matching is only certain between rolls bearing the same batch number. Estimating is made complicated by the fact that lengths and widths of rolls vary. Therefore, you must take the measurements of your room with you and calculate the number of rolls for each wall covering you consider. Dealers will advise you how much to allow for pattern matching with different designs, and usually will estimate for you. It is wise not to skimp as there is always the possibility of a length being spoiled during hanging.

Measure the length of the walls (including doors and windows) and add them together. If you divide by the width of a particular roll, this will tell you the number of lengths (called drops) you need. Measure the height of the ceiling and allow at least 100mm for trimming (or, in the case of repeat patterns, the distance between repeats) and calculate how many drops can be cut from a roll. Divide this number into the number of drops you need and this gives the number of rolls to buy.

For ceilings, decide which direction the lengths will be hung. Then measure how long the lengths will be and add the extra for trimming and pattern matching. Measure the ceiling the other way to calculate how many widths and estimate as for walls.

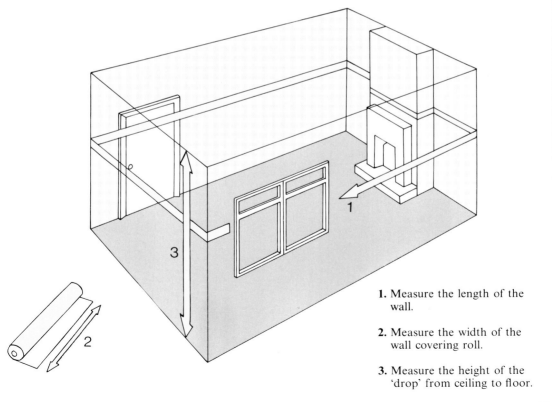

1. Measure the length of the wall.

2. Measure the width of the wall covering roll.

3. Measure the height of the 'drop' from ceiling to floor.

11

Preparing Walls and Ceilings

Begin by removing as much furniture as possible from the room and covering the floor (and remaining furniture) with dust sheets. Then take down all pictures, mirrors and lamps; in fact, anything fixed to the walls. This does not include light switches or wall or ceiling light fixtures.

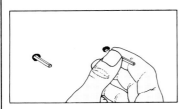

Mark each fixing hole with a matchstick to make it possible to find it later.

Now you need to assess the condition of the surfaces you intend decorating. How much preparation is required depends partly on the wall covering you've chosen. Glossy finishes (especially metallic foil), thin papers and geometric designs show unevenness more than heavy papers and embossed, large patterns.

Removing old wall coverings

As a general rule, old wall coverings should be removed, but if they are sound and firmly stuck to the wall, you can leave them on. However, you can't paper over washable papers, vinyl, or metallic or flocked papers.

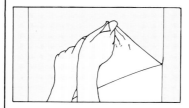

If the previous one is a *vinyl wallpaper*, simply grasp a

corner and peel it off, leaving the backing paper on the wall. This should then be sized after making any repairs to the plaster. Be sure the backing of the old vinyl is adhering well to the wall; otherwise, remove it.

You have a choice of methods of stripping wallpapers, but the idea is the same—to use water to dissolve the old adhesive.

Soak and scrape method: Score the surface of the paper with a stiff wire brush. This is particularly important with washable (i.e. water resistant) and overpainted papers. Next, fill a bucket with warm water and add a little vinegar (this reduces the surface tension of the water and helps it to penetrate the paper). Using a pasting brush, soak the paper as much as you can.

Work on a large area so that you can periodically re-soak the unfinished areas while you're scraping off. Use a stiff scraping knife, being careful not to dig

into the plaster. Keep re-soaking until the paper scrapes off easily, leaving little residue. After stripping, wash off any traces of old paste with clean water.

For stubborn papers, try one of the *chemical wallpaper stripping products*. These cling to the surface and allow more time for the adhesive to soften. Don't confuse these with chemical paint stripper; they are water-based and don't create fumes. However, for papers that have been painted several times you can use a *chemical paint stripper*. Choose one that specifically states that it is designed to strip paper (not only paint), and follow the manufacturers' instructions. Some strippers burn skin, so be sure to wear rubber gloves and also to protect any paintwork that may get splashed. This is a very messy and unpleasant method because of the fumes and should be considered only as a last resort. After stripping, wash down with water to remove all traces of adhesive.

Steam wallpaper strippers are an easier way of removing old wallpapers and are widely available from hire shops. They consist of a pad (rather like a large steam iron) that you hold against the wall with one hand, while scraping the adjacent area with the other. This becomes a continuous operation, and while it takes approximately the same amount of time as soaking and scraping, it involves much less effort and mess. Remember to wash the walls with water afterwards.

Painted walls and ceilings

Provided the paint is sound, painted walls and ceilings should only need washing and, if it is gloss, rubbing down with fine abrasive paper to 'key' the adhesive. If the paint is flaking, scrape off all loose areas, rub down with fine abrasive paper, and apply a coat of primer/sealer to bind the surface. Powdery paint could be distemper or whitewash. If it comes off during washing, remove as much as possible and, when dry, apply a coat of oil based primer/sealer.

New plaster and cement rendering

These need several weeks to dry before decorating. Seal plaster with primer/sealer and cement with masonry sealer before making surface repairs. After sizing, lining paper should be put up unless the covering you are using is very heavy.

Surface repairs

Filling cracks and dents is done with a flexible filling knife and filler as described in the *Tools and Materials* section of this book. Don't be tempted to skip this stage.

Making surface repairs

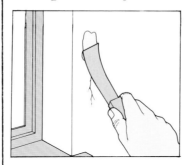

Scoop some filler on to the end of the knife and press the blade flat over the fault, sliding away to leave the filler in the hole. You may need several attempts to ensure the filler is pushed right to the bottom without air being trapped underneath. (If the filler bulges out of the hole, there's an air bubble under it.)

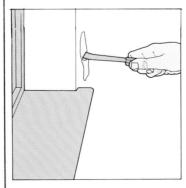

When you've applied enough to fill the hole, hold the knife almost vertically and scrape across the top to remove the excess. Professionals try to clean all the surplus away (including the ridges around the edges), leaving the repair flush. It's worth the extra time spent on the wet filler as rubbing down afterwards is messy, time consuming and hard work.

Large, deep holes should be filled in layers not more than 3mm thick. These dry quickly enough that you can apply a layer every so often while dealing with the small repairs.

This helps with faults that are wider than the filling knife as the surface can be built up gradually around the edges, reducing the area to be scraped off flush. Remember to clean the surplus from around the edges each time you fill.

Very large areas of damaged plaster should be repaired with plaster or one of the DIY plastering systems that is applied by brush. These are used in layers up to 3mm thick and take 24 hours to dry between coats, so, if the fault is deeper than this, use ordinary filler to build up the surface until only a 'skim coat' is needed.

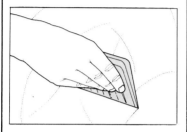

Keep working the surface (re-wetting if necessary) until you're satisfied with the finish.

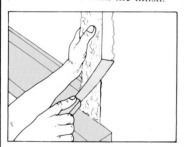

To get a neat edge on outside corners, hold a polythene wrapped piece of wood against one side and flush with the edge. Then fill as if it were a crack. Carefully slide the wood away as the filler sets.

Use a damp sponge to remove the last traces of wet filler from around the repairs.

Size

Surfaces must be smooth, clean, dry and even before putting up wall coverings. Also, you will have to remove excess absorbency that could allow the paste to soak in and cause peeling.

This is done with 'size', and the type of size you should use depends on the type of adhesive you are going to use.

The way to find out which type of size you need is to choose your wall covering first. Then buy the type of adhesive recommended by the manufacturer. The instructions on the adhesive will recommend the type of size to be used. The most common size is a solution of the wallpaper paste and water, but it isn't suitable for all adhesives, so follow the manufacturers' instructions.

If surfaces have been treated for dampness (e.g. with waterproof paints or foil vapour barriers) be sure to read the instructions on these products. They often specify that only heavy duty adhesives containing fungicide should be used over them.

Size is applied by simply brushing on with a pasting brush or large paint brush. Coat evenly and brush out thoroughly to avoid lumps. The important thing is to follow the instructions concerning drying time. The size must be dry before applying the wall covering. Hanging the paper too soon (or leaving sizing out altogether) is a common cause of problems later. Using size correctly prevents the surface absorbing the adhesive too quickly and allows more time to reposition the wall covering.

Lining paper

Lining paper can be used to prepare walls and ceilings either for wall coverings or for painting, and you should use the correct paper for the job. Standard lining paper is used with wall coverings and a non-absorbent finish paper for painting, although it is possible to paint over standard paper.

Overall, lining a room has three advantages: it improves the final result; it is an easier surface on which to hang wall coverings; and it gives you the chance to make a few mistakes without spoiling the job. Having worked your way around the room once, you will know the likely trouble spots.

The purpose of lining paper is to provide a surface that is consistent in texture and has a uniform colour. This can be especially important when there is discoloured plaster and filler on the walls.

Lining paper comes in several weights, the heaviest giving the most improvement to flaws in the surface. However, cracks should still be filled to give as smooth a surface as possible.

Medium weight lining paper is the easiest wall covering to hang and, as such, is the best introduction to basic wallpapering for beginners.

Before starting, choose the type of wall covering you will apply over the lining paper, as you must use a size and adhesive that is suitable for the top covering—not just the lining paper. For instance, if the top covering is going to be a washable paper, the manufacturer will specify a heavy duty paste containing fungicide.

Lining paper on walls

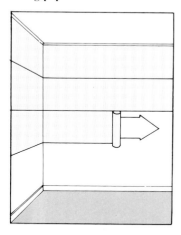

Lining paper is usually hung at right angles to the top wall covering, i.e. horizontally on walls, to avoid any chance of the joins between strips of lining paper falling in the same place as the joins in the top covering.

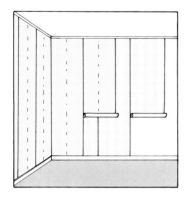

If you are wallpapering for the first time, it is easier to hang paper vertically on walls. But you must plan the joins carefully not to coincide with the top covering by starting in a different part of the room.

Lining paper on ceilings

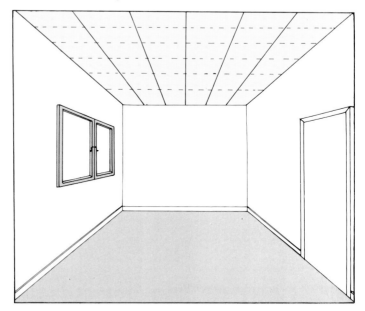

Ceilings should be decorated (whether painted or papered) first, to stop drips and splashes from spoiling finished work on the walls.

As ceilings are slightly more difficult than walls, you may choose to paint the ceiling and confine your first project to the walls. Alternatively, you can line the ceiling and walls and then decide whether to paint or paper the ceiling.

The correct starting point for the finished wall covering on ceilings is parallel to the window side of the room, working strip by strip toward the door.

You should put up the lining paper at right angles to this, but, if it would mean very long lengths (in a long narrow room for instance), put it up in the same direction. Remember to ensure the joins don't coincide with the top covering by starting in a different place. If the ceiling is to be painted after lining, hang the paper in the correct direction as this is the top covering.

Lining paper is hung by the same method as wallpaper (see next section).

Use the right paste and size for the top wall covering, not just the lining paper.

If you haven't hung wallpaper before, try starting with a medium grade lining paper to get some practice and improve the final result.

Papering Ceilings

Begin by assembling the tools, materials, and steps and ladders you will need: pasting table, pasting brush, seam roller, hanging brush, adhesive (correctly mixed), plumb line, chalk line, shears, damp cloth or sponge and clean water to rinse it in, sharp knife, steel straight edge, measuring tape, pencil, and an apron or clean dry cloth is useful for wiping your hands and the shears while hanging.

Now is the time to unwrap all the rolls of wallpaper to check for colour matching and faults.

Where to begin

Set up your working platform at the window end of the room. Working from the source of light towards the entrance of a room minimizes the appearance of the joins between strips.

Measure the width of the roll of paper and mark the ceiling either side at a distance 10mm less than this from the end wall. Fix one end of a chalk line with a nail or drawing pin to one of the marks and hold the line taut against the other mark. Then pull the line straight down with your other hand and let it snap back against the ceiling. (See illustration on page 5.) It should leave a distinct straight line of chalk that will

be the guide for the first length of paper. Remove the line and the nail.

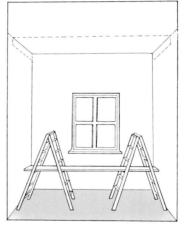

Measure the distance across the ceiling, adding approximately 100mm at each end to be trimmed off once the strip is up. This is the length of the first strip of wallpaper. If the room is regularly shaped, you should cut the remaining lengths at the same time to speed the work. Be sure to allow enough extra length on each piece for matching if there is a pattern on the paper. Also, if the pattern is large, take the time to measure the first length on the face of the paper to make sure the design will be well placed on the ceiling.

Pasting and folding

Lay the first length face down, on the pasting table, overlapping the far edge of the table by 10mm or so. Hold the end down with one hand or put something on it to keep it from rolling up.

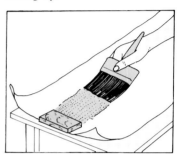

Apply a brushful of paste down the centre of the paper to make it lie flat, and then brush it evenly up to and over the edge of the overhang, always from the centre outwards. It is important to coat all of the paper, as dry spots will show later as bubbles, and areas too heavily coated will cause a bulge.

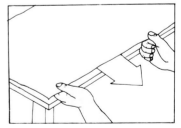

When the far side is well pasted, slide the paper to the near side of the table, overlapping as before, and repeat. Be careful not to allow any paste to stray on to the table as it will mar the face of the paper.

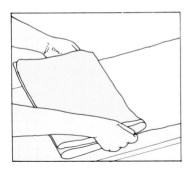

When the paper on the table is evenly and thoroughly covered, fold over approximately 30cm from the end (paste to paste) and lift this on to the next 30cm, continuing to the unpasted area.

Paste and fold the remainder of the length in the same way. Try to keep the folds even as it makes the length easier to handle.

The instructions supplied with the adhesive or wallpaper will state whether the paper must be left for a few minutes after pasting, but it is important not to allow it to become tacky or it will then be difficult to slide the paper into position. Once you know how much time it takes to hang one length, you can work out a routine so that one length is always pasted and ready to be hung.

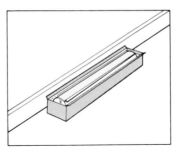

Ready pasted papers should be cut to length and soaked in the tray supplied with them for the length of time recommended in the instructions. Then, instead of folding, you can leave it rolled up to be unrolled a little at a time, as you put it up.

Hanging the paper

Have the hanging brush and shears ready to hand but be careful of placing shears in a front pocket as they can be dangerous when you are climing on and off the platform.

The platform should be directly under the chalk line on the ceiling to hang the first two lengths. Then it should be moved after each length. This way you are always directly under the important edge of the paper, i.e. the side that is being aligned with the previous length.

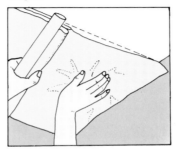

Place a roll of paper or a cardboard tube under the

pasted and folded length and hold all the folds except the top one with your thumb. This must be held near the ceiling with one hand while positioning and smoothing each fold in turn with the other.

Open the top fold and carefully align the edge with the chalk mark, leaving the 100mm overlap at the wall, and smooth with the hanging brush from the middle outwards to remove bubbles. If you need to slide the paper, do it with the flat of your hand (not just fingertips) to avoid tearing it.

When the first fold is properly positioned and smooth, release the next fold from under your thumb and move along to put it in place and smooth with the brush as before.

It is especially important to keep the edge of the first length straight on the chalk mark. Curves in the edges will become worse with each length afterwards.

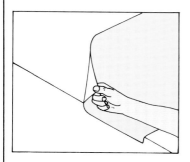

Try not to pull on one side or the other as this may stretch the paper out of true; slide it and, if necessary, peel off a little and replace in the correct position.

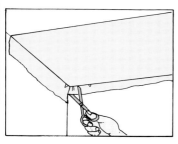

When the first length is in position, make a small cut at each of the corners where the paper overlaps the two walls.

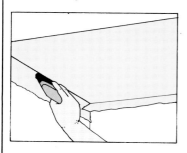

Use the brush to press the 100mm overlap into the corner along one side of the length. Then brush the overlap at each end into the corner.

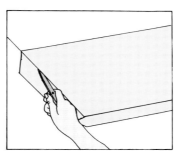

Use the rounded tips of the blades of the shears to gently crease the paper into the corner.

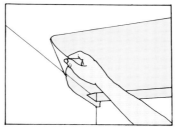

Then peel back enough of the paper to allow you to cut along about 10mm from the crease mark. If the walls aren't going to be papered, cut along the crease mark to leave the paper neatly finished up to the wall. Brush the paper back into place.

Paper the remainder of the ceiling in the same way, each length butting up to the previous one, not overlapping.

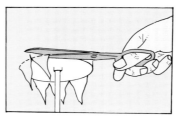

When you come to a light fitting, pierce the paper with the

shears and make cuts outward so the paper can be creased around the base of the fitting. Peel back each piece and trim along the crease as before.

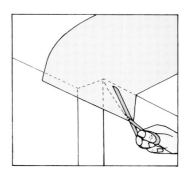

When the end or side of a length falls at the corner of an alcove, hang the paper up to the obstruction and make a diagonal cut up to the corner as shown.

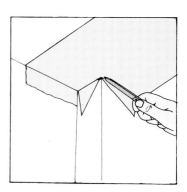

Then crease and trim each edge separately.

The last length probably won't be full width. If the strip of ceiling remaining to be papered is much narrower than the width of the paper, it should be cut to manageable size before pasting and hanging.

Papering Walls

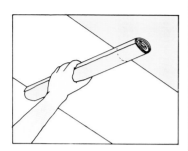

Hold a rolled up length of paper between the wall and edge of the previous length at the widest point, and allow approximately 25mm extra for trimming.

Lightweight papers can be cut loosely folded, but heavier ones may need to be laid out and cut down the full length.

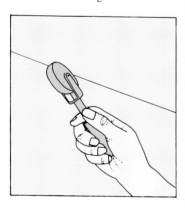

As the paste is setting go over the joins with a seam roller to make sure they are firmly stuck. Embossed papers can be dented by a seam roller; use the hanging brush instead.

Any air bubbles that do not seem to be disappearing as the paper dries should be pierced with a pin and the area brushed down. Be careful that paste doesn't come out of the pin hole and get picked up by the brush.

Where to begin

Deciding where to start papering the walls of a room depends partly on the pattern (if any) on the chosen paper.

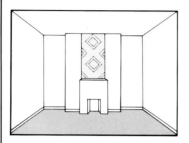

A large, bold motif or a geometric pattern should be centred at the focal point of the room. This may be the chimney breast or the centre of the most important wall, for instance. Also, there should be a complete pattern or motif near the top of the wall. Once the first length is hung, work outward from both sides.

If your paper has a *small pattern* or is *plain* simply hang the first length on the most important wall and follow the rule of working from the source of the light toward the door.

As it will almost certainly be impossible to match the pattern

on the last length, arrange to finish in the least important corner of the room (a doorway near the corner of two walls, perhaps).

Using the plumb line

Start by striking a chalk line as on the ceiling, except this time you must use a plumb line to make it vertical. Don't trust the side of a window or door frame to be straight enough.

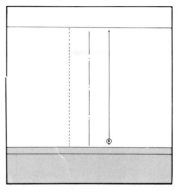

Near the top of the wall, measure the centre of the area where you will hang the first length. Then mark the wall to one side half the width of your paper. Tie the plumb line (rubbed with chalk) to a nail driven at this mark. Make sure the nail is long enough to allow the plumb bob to swing without touching the wall.

When the bob is hanging motionless, hold the line at the bottom taut against the wall with one hand and pull the middle of the line away from the wall with the other. Then let it snap back into place, leaving a straight, vertical line of chalk on the wall. This is the mark to guide the edge of the first length.

Pasting and Folding

Cut the first length (allowing 50mm extra top and bottom) to position the pattern as you want, and lay it face down on the pasting table overlapping the far edge by 10mm or so. Hold down the end with one hand or place something on it to keep it from rolling up.

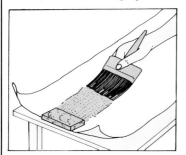

Apply a brushful of paste down the centre to hold it flat and brush the paste out and over the far edge. Slide the paper over the near side of the table and paste that side. Make sure the edges are well covered. Wipe off any paste that gets on to the table to prevent it from spoiling the face of the paper.

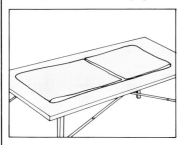

When you have pasted as much of the length as you can, fold the end (paste to paste) over to the centre of the length and slide the remainder of the paper on to the table and paste as before.

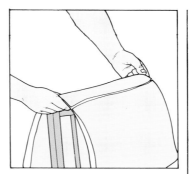

If the instructions supplied with the paper or adhesive state that the paper should be left for a few minutes after pasting, fold the other end over to the centre and hang the length over a chair. Once the first length is hung, you may paste two lengths and then hang one and paste one alternately, so there is always one length pasted and waiting.

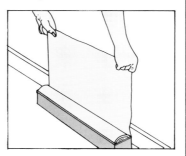

For *ready pasted papers*, soak the length in the tray for the length of time stated in the instructions. Then place the tray on the floor where the length will be hung and simply lift the paper out by the top edge. Allow the rest of the length to unroll in the trough so that any excess water can drain back into the trough. Hang the paper in position and smooth out on the wall.

Hanging the paper

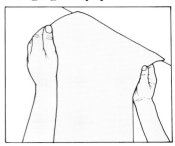

Open the top half of the folded first length and hold it up in line with the chalk mark. Overlap the ceiling by approximately 50mm.

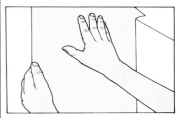

Put one hand in the middle near the top of the paper and slide the length into position. Remember to use the flat of your hand, not just fingertips.

Use the hanging brush down the middle and toward the edge and adjust the paper, if necessary, to keep it to the line. Once you are satisfied with the positioning, smooth the paper to the wall with the brush, always working from the middle toward the edges.

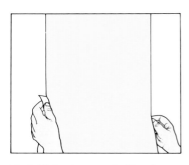

Unfold the bottom half and continue. Beware of paste squeezing out from under the edge and being picked up by the brush. Wipe the brush frequently on your apron or a cloth.

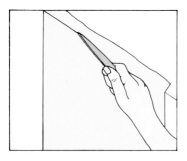

Once the whole length is firmly smoothed to the wall, use the round tip of the shears to crease gently into the corner along the top.

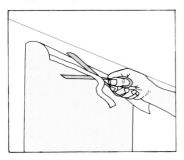

Peel back the top, cut carefully along the crease and brush it

back into place to finish neatly to the ceiling. Repeat at the bottom. Wipe off any excess paste immediately from the ceiling and skirting board.

If the ceiling has paper that isn't water resistant (washable), be careful not to let the pasted side of the wallpaper touch it. Leave a small overlap and don't push it into the corner until you are going to trim it. That way you can hold the end of the paper away from the ceiling while creasing it.

Measure the next length by putting the roll on the floor. Hold the end of the paper up to the wall until there is enough overlap at the top and, if necessary, the pattern matches the first length. If the next possible pattern match means having an overlap at the top of approximately half a length, this is called a 'half drop and repeat' pattern, and you should use two rolls of paper, cutting a length from each one alternately. Otherwise there will be too much waste. If you wish, you may cut all the lengths for the room before beginning to paste and hang them.

Coping with Obstructions

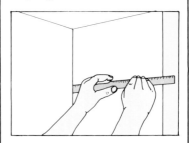

Inside corners: Measure the distance between the edge of the last full width and the corner at the widest point. Allow an extra 25mm and cut a length to this width.

Paste and hang the piece with the overlap going around the corner, being sure to brush the paper well into the corner.

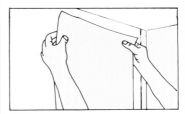

Hold the length of paper you cut off the last piece up to the corner, as shown, and mark the wall 5mm further away from the corner at the top and bottom of the wall. If the piece you cut off is too narrow, use a full width piece.

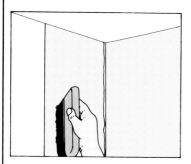

Using the plumb line as before, mark the wall with a chalk line using the mark that is furthest from the corner as a guide. Paste and hang this length to the chalk line, with the other edge overlapping the first length. Now you can continue hanging, knowing the new lengths will be straight and vertical.

Outside corners: You should not fold a length around an outside corner as walls are seldom vertical or straight.

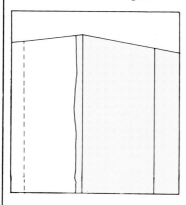

Follow the same procedure as for internal corners, trimming a length to overlap the corner by 25mm. Plumb a new line on the adjacent wall so the second part overlaps the first, as near the corner as possible.

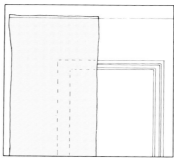

Door and window frames: Hang the top portion of the length as usual and let the paper fall over the frame.

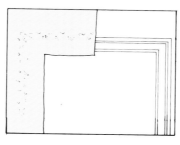

Cut around the frame leaving at least 50mm too much paper overlapping. Then press the paper gently onto the top corner of the frame and dent it slightly.

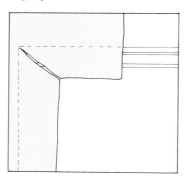

Make a diagonal cut to the mark made by the corner.

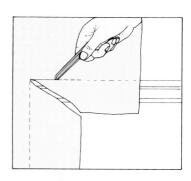

Now you can brush the top edge into the corner on the top of the frame and crease it with the shears.

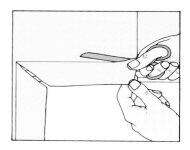

Peel the edge away and be careful not to tear the paper at the corner. Trim along the crease.

Hang the rest of the length along the edge all the way down, and push the paper onto the bottom corner of the frame

22

(if it is a window frame). Make a diagonal cut as you did for the top corner and brush down, crease, and trim the edge down the side of the frame (all the way to the skirting board if it is a door frame).

Light switches: Begin as usual, allowing the paper to hang over the switch.

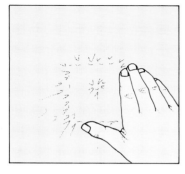

When enough of the length is smoothed to hold it to the wall, press the paper gently onto the switch, peel it back and pierce the centre with the shears.

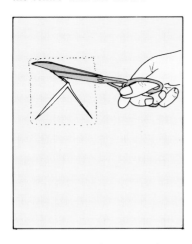

Make a diagonal cut to each corner of the indent on the

paper if the switch cover is square, or several cuts if it is round.

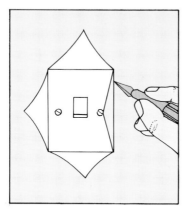

Crease each flap against the edge of the switch cover and trim with a sharp knife.

Be careful cutting the paper as it tears easily when damp, and wipe any paste from the knife after each cut.

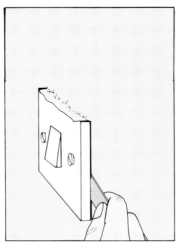

If you first turn off the electricity at the main switch, you can cut each flap a little too long, loosen the bolts

holding the switch cover, and push the edges under it. Don't leave more than 3mm of paper underneath the switch cover. Don't do this if you are using metal foil paper and *always turn off the electricity*.

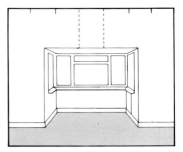

Bay windows and reveals: Using a pencil and a roll of paper as a guide to the width of each strip, mark out where lengths will fall on a wall that has a bay window or window reveal (recessed into the wall). There must be a length either side of the recess that can be folded around the corner. Usually the solution is to centre a length over the reveal and work outwards to either side.

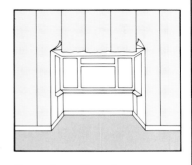

Paper the wall as shown, leaving the short lengths untrimmed. Then paper the ceiling of the bay allowing 25mm overlap up the wall under the short lengths.

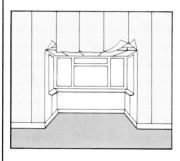

Brush them down (applying fresh paste if it has dried in the meantime) and trim off to the corner.

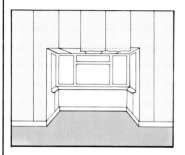

You can use a straight edge and pencil to lightly mark a straight line and then cut with shears.

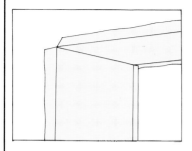

Shallow reveals may be papered inside first, with a small overlap onto the wall around the edges. Then paper the wall as usual, trimming the lengths up to the corners.

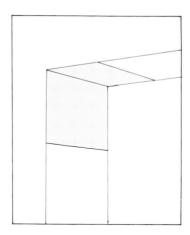

For a *very shallow reveal* (say 150mm deep), you may be able to fold the lengths from the wall into it. In this case, cut and paste a small piece of paper into the top corners, as shown.

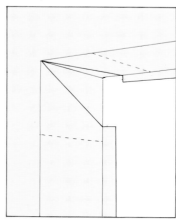

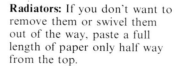

This will make sure there isn't a small area of bare wall left at the corners.

Radiators: If you don't want to remove them or swivel them out of the way, paste a full length of paper only half way from the top.

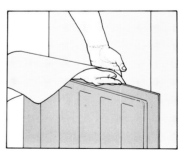

Hang this length as far as pasted and, with the bottom folded face to face, push the paper down behind the radiator as far as the brackets.

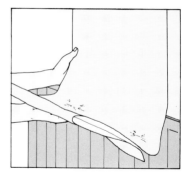

Crease the paper on the brackets and pull the paper out again.

Make a cut from the bottom up to each crease and a diagonal cut to each corner as shown.

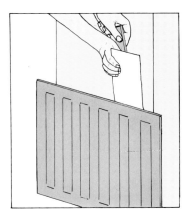

Then, holding the bottom of the length up to the wall, paste the remainder and brush it down behind the radiator. A cloth wrapped around a piece of wood or wire may help to smooth down the paper where you can't reach it.

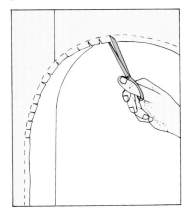

Arches: Paper the wall first, allowing 25mm overlap at the edges of the arch, and make cuts in from the edge of the overlap every 25mm or so, as shown. Fold these flaps around the corner and smooth them down well. Trim off any edges that overlap to keep the edge neat.

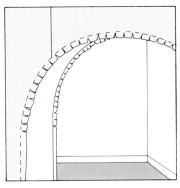

If the arch is a *doorway*, paper the other wall, if desired.

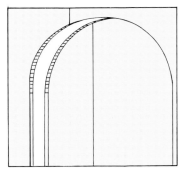

If the arch is a *recess*, paper the back wall area, keeping the pattern matching the lengths above, and allowing a 10mm overlap at the sides and top of the arch.

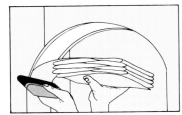

Finish with a strip of paper around the inside. Cut the strip carefully as it won't be possible to trim it once hung.

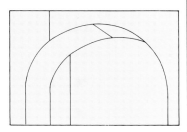

If the pattern would look wrong upside down, use two strips joined at the top. Overlap the ends of the two strips 25mm or so, and use a steel rule and sharp knife to cut through both layers at once. Remove the offcuts and smooth down the ends to finish neatly.

Stairwells and high walls: Pay particular attention to the safety of your working platforms. Take up stair carpets.

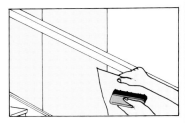

Remove hand rails that are fitted to side walls, if possible. If the rail is touching the wall you can trim the paper above and below as separate lengths, but ensure they are lined up. Very long lengths of lightweight paper may tear under their own weight when being hung, so choose a heavy paper or vinyl covering, or get a helper to support the folded length while you hang from the top. On side walls of stair wells, hang the longest length first to a plumbed chalk line.

Hanging Other Wall Coverings

Vinyls are hung in the same way as paper. They are easier in that they don't tear and paste can be wiped off without marring the face. Care must be taken to push them well into corners and around edges as they are less supple than paper and can tend to spring back.

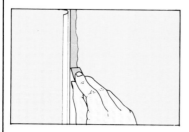

Remember that vinyls need specific adhesives for hanging and also a special glue to stick overlaps. This must be used with care to prevent it touching the surface where it would show.

Paper backed fabrics such as hessian, felt, wool strand, silk, woven grasses, and suede need very careful hanging as the surfaces are spoiled by adhesive or even by water marks. If in doubt, try a small area before deciding. Adhesives and techniques vary and each manufacturer supplies instructions for joins, overlaps etc. Remember that sunlight affects these materials. Also, use them only where there is little likelihood of their being touched.

Un-backed fabrics can be applied to walls using techniques that fall outside the scope of this book. These include stapling to wooden battens or one of the track systems made for the purpose.

Metal foils are also very delicate, both during and after hanging. Adhesive (usually two coats) must be applied to the wall, not the foil. A short pile roller is used as brush marks would show in the surface. Also, the bristles of a hanging brush would dent the surface, so it must be smoothed with a soft felt or smooth rubber roller. There must be no lumps in the adhesive and, of course, the surface beneath must be absolutely smooth. Lengths should be butt joined and unsightly overlaps may be cut through using a steel straight edge and sharp knife as described earlier.

Apart from tearing, the biggest problem with foil is that it creases. Practise on a small area free of awkward corners before attempting a room. Metal foils can be very effectively used as features on panels (perhaps with borders) or one wall to create a feeling of space. Buy pre-trimmed foil as it is time-consuming cutting selvedges, and joins are more difficult.

Selvedges may be trimmed before hanging or by cutting through both layers of an overlap, but this is a long job.

A note of warning—metal foils conduct electricity, so switch off at the main switch before trimming around light fittings, switches, and sockets. *Don't remove switch covers and insert foil under them.*

Wood veneer is available on a heavy backing of canvas, either pre-finished or ready to be sealed. As you would imagine, it is much less pliable than paper, often coming in panels, rather than rolls, and sometimes numbered to match the grain of adjacent lengths. As joins will show and overlapping is impossible, it is best to use it on plain walls without many awkward corners or obstructions.

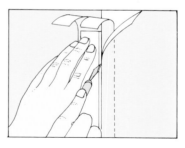

It can be folded around corners and butt joined to the next length by cutting through both at once.

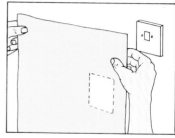

Lengths must be offered up to the wall repeatedly and

trimmed to final shape and size before hanging. This includes switches and wall sockets, etc.

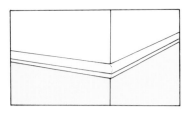

If you decide to partially cover a wall with one of these, a border of wood moulding may be used to finish the edge.

Cork is made in rolls on a paper backing, pre-finished and washable. It is not much more difficult to hang than a heavy paper or vinyl, but, to look effective, joins must be as unobtrusive as possible and, of

course, they can be no overlaps. Be sure to buy pre-trimmed.

Glass fibre is useful for badly cracked walls as it helps hold the surface together. Use the paste specified by the manufacturer. Trimming can only be done when the material is dry, i.e. before it contacts the adhesive, and each join must be cut through both layers.

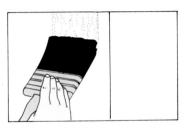

After marking the wall where the joins will be, paste the wall

leaving 25mm free of paste down each side.

Hang the first length and paste the wall where the second length will be.

Overlap the next length by 25mm and cut through both layers.

Remove the offcuts and smooth down with a roller.

SPECIAL EFFECTS

Left *Pages of magazines or newspapers can be hung in the same way as wallpaper.*

Below left *This simply-constructed table has been covered with a left-over roll of wallpaper. If you want to copy this idea, make sure that the design is suitable. A large, repeating design would not work as well.*

Below *Here are two striking patterns of vinyl wall covering with the joins hidden by borders. Smaller borders have been used to finish the edges of the doors and the bottom of the wall.*

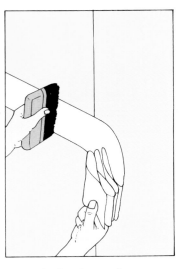

Left Using the same wall coverings on doors and other flat surfaces is an inexpensive way of adding a designer touch.

Borders may be used to divide walls and ceilings and create the effect of cornices, picture rails and dadoes. The main thing to remember is that they must be hung straight as any inaccuracy will spoil the effect. You should always snap a chalk line for each length of border. This includes horizontal and vertical. It is best to ask a helper to hold the other end of the line as you won't want to drive nails into the newly papered walls.

lining paper or newspaper and place the border, face down, as shown. Brush on the paste, allowing it to overlap onto the paper beneath. Take care not to move the strip.

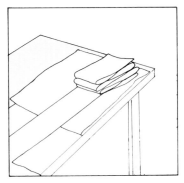

When you have pasted as much of the strip as you can, fold it as you would for a ceiling and place it down on a different part of the table, as shown. This way the paste won't spoil the face of the strip. Of course, you must cover the table with fresh paper for each strip you paste.

Hang the borders as for wallpaper, but place them in position carefully to avoid marring the wall covering with paste.

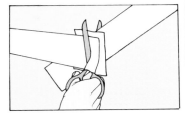

Where two strips meet, join them this way. Placing a sheet of paper between, overlap the ends and cut through both strips at once with the shears, as shown. Remove the offcuts and smooth down the ends.

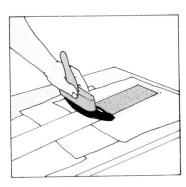

When pasting narrow strips, cover the pasting table with

TOP TEN TIPS

1. Always choose the type of wall covering you will use *before* preparing the room and buying the adhesive or size. There may be specific instructions on the wall covering stating which adhesives and sizes must be used for lining paper or surface preparation.

2. Always check the batch numbers (if any) on the rolls are the same before you unwrap them. Then, on the table, roll quickly through each one to make sure there are no faults.

3. Follow the manufacturers' instructions regarding mixing of adhesives. When mixing cold water paste, always add the powder slowly to the correct amount of clean water, stirring constantly. This avoids lumps in the paste that would show in the finished job.

4. A string tied across the paste bucket makes a convenient place to rest the brush when it's not being used. You can also use the string to wipe any excess paste off the brush.

5. If you're a beginner, try hanging a medium-weight lining paper before attempting the final covering. This will give you a 'practice run' and also improve the finished job.

6. Plan the whole job first. Never let the joins in the top wall covering coincide with the joins in the lining paper or any old wall covering beneath.

7. Keep paste off the table by overlapping the wall covering 10mm on one side and then the other. Be sure the edges are well pasted. Brush outwards. When pasting narrow strips or borders, cover the table with clean lining paper. Place the strip on a clean piece each time you paste and change the lining paper when it's used up.
Use a roll of the wall covering (or lining paper) and a pencil to mark the wall or ceiling where the widths will be.

When lining the room first, use a different coloured pencil to mark where the widths of lining paper will be.

Below A cool and light bedroom with colour co-ordinated paper and fabrics.

8. Wallpaper should be left to soften for a few minutes after pasting. When pasting lengths of paper, paste two at the start. Then, hang the first drop and, before hanging the second, paste the third one. That way, there is always one length waiting while you're hanging the previous one.

9. Save some of the leftover wall covering to use for repairs later.

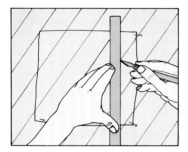

Place a piece of paper over the damaged area (making sure to match any pattern) and secure it down in position with pins. Cut through both layers with a sharp knife and metal rule. Cut a shape that will show the edges least.

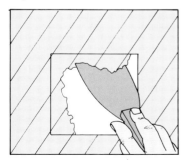

Remove the patch and carefully scrape away the area of damaged paper inside the cut lines.

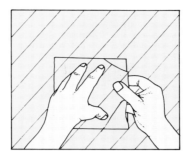

Paste the new patch and place it on the repair carefully to avoid squeezing paste out at the edges.

10. Here's a way to repair light and medium weight papers.

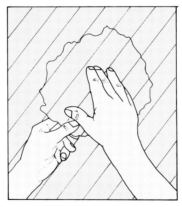

From a spare piece, tear out a piece large enough to cover the damage. Make it irregularly shaped and feather the edges so they are as thin as possible. Place the piece over the damage so that the pattern matches and see that the edges are as hidden as possible. Keep tearing the edges until you're satisfied with the match. Then paste the patch and put it on. Line it up without sliding it and be careful not to let paste from the edges smear the paper.

Safety Tips

1. Some adhesives and pastes containing fungicides are poisonous. Wash them off your skin immediately. Don't leave a bucket, brush or even the stick used to stir it where children or pets may find them. That goes for sharp tools, too.

2. All products that could be harmful if contacted or swallowed usually have recommended first aid treatment printed on the packaging in case of accidents. Read them *before* they could become necessary.

3. Take the time to set up ladders and scaffolding safely. Don't leave them alone if there's a chance children may play on them.

4. Don't carry a trimming knife or shears in a front pocket. You can stab yourself when stepping up on to the ladder or if you stumble.

5. Always switch off electricity at the main switch *before* removing light fittings or switch covers.

6. Metal foil coverings conduct electricity. Never insert the edges under switch covers.

Author
Dek Messecar
Series Consultant Editor
Bob Tattersall
Design
Mike Rose and Bob Lamb
Picture Research
Ann Lyons
Illustrations
Rob Shone
Rick Blakely
Anne Lamb

Dek Messecar is a professional joiner who has had experience on all aspects of DIY.

Bob Tattersall has been a DIY journalist for over 25 years and was editor of *Homemaker* for 16 years. He now works as a freelance journalist and broadcaster. Regular contact with the main DIY manufacturers keeps him up-to-date on all new products and developments. He has written many books on various aspects of DIY and, while he is considered 'an expert', he prefers to think of himself as a do-it-yourselfer who happens to be a journalist.

Photographs from Elizabeth Whiting Photo Library

Cover photography by Carl Warner

The *Do It! Series* was conceived, edited and designed by Elizabeth Whiting & Associates and Robert Lamb & Company for William Collins Sons and Co Ltd

First published 1983 by William Collins Sons and Co Ltd
Reprinted 1983, 1986, 1987 (twice)

Revised edition first published by HarperCollins*Publishers* 1989
Reprinted 1992, 1995
9 8 7 6 5 4 3

ISBN 0 00 411894 4

Printed in Hong Kong